QUARRIES
Health and Safety 1982–83

(and other premises to which the Mines and Quarries Act
1954 does not apply)

LONDON: HER MAJESTY'S STATIONERY OFFICE

Any enquiries regarding this publication should be addressed to the
Health and Safety Executive at any area office or the Public Enquiry
Point, St Hugh's House, Stanley Precinct, Bootle, Merseyside, L20 3QY
tel 051–951 4381.

ISBN 0 11 883793 1

Contents

Foreword

This report is, for the first time, biennial but is supported by annual reports from each of the Inspectorate districts. The message of all these reports is that in the vast majority of investigations the cause of accidents is found to be repetitive year after year and that many could have been avoided by more care and attention, either by individuals or by better supervision and organisation.

Safety is not the sole prerogative of a mystical 'they' who 'should do something about it'. It is a joint affair involving designers, manufacturers, employers and employees and is a field in which there is a need for persistent effort, for application to detail and for a will to succeed. This report and other literature concerning health and safety at work provides the building materials for a safer environment but all those involved in the work activity must build that environment.

It is to be hoped that lessons will be learnt from perusal of the report and that the next biennial report will record long lasting improvements.

A HARLEY
HM Chief Inspector of Mines and Quarries

Summary

1 This report reviews safety and health in quarries, landfill sites, peat workings, on-shore exploratory drilling sites and ready mix concrete dry batch plants located on quarry premises. It covers the period 1982–83, two years with a marked difference in the number of accidents reported annually. During those two years 24 accidents were reported which resulted in fatalities and 208 which resulted in major injury. District reports continue to be compiled on a yearly basis and a more detailed account of specific accidents is recorded in them. Copies are available on request from the Principal District Inspector of Mines and Quarries in charge of each Inspectorate District.

2 The general message of the report continues to be similar to that of previous years in that sustained effort must continue to be put into health and safety to obtain worthwhile and lasting improvements. The means of carrying the message forward are available through technical institutions, safety committees and trade associations. It is encouraging, for instance, to see the strong support given to the quarry plant exhibitions which were held, on different sites, in 1982 and 1983. These presented an opportunity for users and manufacturers to meet and discuss operational problems in which safety forms an important part. However, it is in the quarry itself that the real effort has to be made with the full involvement and active co-operation of everyone, management and employees.

Quarries

General

3 At the end of 1983, 3371 quarries were operating and workmen's inspectors carried out 490 inspections under Section 123 of the Mines and Quarries Act 1954. Apart from an increase around 1976/77 the number of Section 123 workmen's inspections has gradually decreased since their introduction in 1958 as shown in Table 1. Figures are not available for inspections made by safety representatives under the Safety Representatives and Safety Committee Regulations 1976, but it is hoped that these more than compensate for the reduction in Section 123 inspections. Trade Unions have a part to play in this case by encouraging their membership to take an active part in inspections of the workplace.

Table 1 Section 123: Workmen's inspections at quarries

Five-year period	Annual average
1958/62	725
1963/67	517
1968/72	317
1973/77	306
1978/82	337

Accidents

4 During the two years the number of accidents reported (fatal and major injury) were 217 compared to 200 in the previous two-year period. A comparison of totals for five-year periods gives a better indication of trends and the average number of accidents over such periods for the past 20 years shows an encouraging decline. The increase in major injuries in 1979/83 is due to the change in reporting procedures when the Notification of Accidents and Dangerous Occurrences Regulations came into force in January 1981 and this must be taken into account when making comparison. The figures, together with other accident statistics, are given in Figs 1 and 2 and in the Appendix.

Falls of ground

5 Accidents in this category resulted in two persons being killed and five seriously injured. Both fatalities involved drivers who had dismounted from their vehicles relatively close to a working face and were then struck by falling material. The causes of all the accidents emphasised the necessity of a thorough inspection of every face before work is started and also periodically throughout the shift. Any changes or signs of movement should be recorded in the daily report together with the remedial action taken and it is important that disused faces, which border haul roads or are adjacent to working areas, should be included. The quarry face should be examined after every primary blast to check for changes in the face structure which may affect stability as massive movements have occurred in the past due to failure to appreciate the significance of small variations in the type of rock. Where doubt exists, further technical advice should be sought and possibly, exploratory bore holes drilled to prove the deposit behind the suspect area.

Explosives

6 One person was killed and two seriously injured in accidents involving projected material from shot firing operations.

7 While the Quarries Explosives Regulations 1959 require the shot firer to determine the danger zone likely to be created by a shot and to ensure that no persons are in that zone unless they have taken proper shelter, it is wise, where practicable, for the manager to make it a rule that all persons in the quarry take shelter during shot firing operations.

Haulage and transport

8   There were 97 accidents involving haulage and transport including conveyors. Fourteen were fatal and this figure accounts for 61% of total fatalities over the two-year period. Many were repetitive in that they occurred in circumstances which had led to very similar accidents in the past and to which attention had been drawn in previous annual reports and publications. Far more effort needs to be made in all operational aspects of quarry vehicles to achieve a reduction in the number of accidents in this category. Statistics for haulage and transport accidents, excluding those involving conveyors, are shown for one and five-year periods in Figs 1 and 2 and are classified by type and location in Fig 3.

9   Operations involving the use of quarry vehicles resulted in 75 of these accidents, 10 of which had fatal consequences.

10   Over the years there have been a number of accidents involving tipmen and one was killed during 1982 when struck by a large lump of clay falling from a reversing dump truck. The very nature of a tipman's job requires him to work in a potentially hazardous area in close proximity to large vehicles with restricted driver visibility. Management at a number of coal quarries have now successfully modified their system of work, by use of two way radio for example, to obviate the necessity for tipmen. Managers are urged to closely examine the operations at their quarries and, wherever possible, take similar action.

11   Twenty of the major injury accidents occurred during work associated with maintenance, repair or inspection of quarry vehicles. In one, an experienced bulldozer driver was killed, while attempting to locate one of the angling arms in the blade bracket on his machine, when struck on the head by the violent upward movement of the arm. The upper tilting brace had been connected and this exerted a force on the pin connecting the angling arm to the bulldozer frame. When an attempt was made to lever up the angling arm, to connect with the blade, the change in geometry was such that the arm moved suddenly with great force. When an angling arm is fitted on these machines it should first be connected to the bulldozer blade and then to the machine frame. This procedure should be reversed when disconnecting the arm. Figure 4 shows details.

12   Maintenance and repair work of large items of plant frequently involves the handling of heavy, cumbersome parts or requires work to be carried out in cramped surroundings. Many accidents could be avoided had an appraisal been made of the work to be carried out and arrangements made to provide suitable lifting equipment and temporary working platforms. Maintenance work involving fitting wheels and tyres has resulted in a number of accidents over the years and these operations are further discussed in the mechanical engineering section.

13   Two men were killed in separate accidents during towing operations on gradients of 1:4 and 1:6 respectively, which demonstrates that gradients where vehicles have to travel should, where practicable, be less than 1:10. Also the layout and design of the

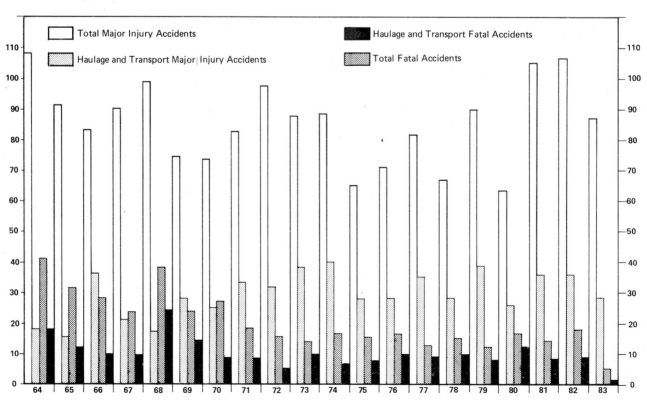

Fig 1   Quarry accidents, 1964–83

excavations should be such that the necessity to tow vehicles is not a regular part of the production process. There may be exceptional occasions, when towing is a necessity, but this operation should be done in accordance with instructions incorporated in the manager's vehicle rules.

14   For example, a rigid towbar with adequate connecting points should be used; steps should be taken to ensure that the towing vehicle is suitable for the duty; the surface of the route to be followed should be suitable and the vehicle to be towed should be in a safe condition. One quarry has a commendable scheme for towing dump trucks and other large vehicles when the engines are inoperative. A small diesel-driven hydraulic pump is placed on a steel mounting plate fitted to each vehicle and the pump provides hydraulic power for the steering. The towing truck is fitted with a flexible hose coupled to an air compressor and to the failed vehicle so that the brakes, audible warning and other services are energised.

15   Restricted visibility from the driving position is a feature of many quarry vehicles and was a contributory cause of eight reportable accidents including three fatalities. The ideal solution has not yet been found but attention should be given to fitting well designed rear view mirrors, placing static mirrors in operating areas and more widespread adoption of the various visibility aids and sensors currently available. Layout of traffic flow should also be examined with the object of reducing reversing to a minimum and, whenever possible, to maintaining a one way traffic system.

Conveyors

16   Twenty-two accidents occurred during work associated with belt conveyors. In the past 15 years 23 persons have been killed and 112 seriously injured in similar accidents but, despite a considerable amount of publicity, it is apparent that the hazards are still not fully appreciated. One requisite is a high standard of guarding and BS 2890 provides good guidance in this respect but, it is also imperative that guards are correctly maintained and are kept in position whenever the conveyor is running. However, as a large proportion of accidents occur when guards are removed for maintenance and spillage clearance, attention must be paid to the design and installation of the conveyor system to minimise the need to remove guards. A solution adopted in one quarry following a fatality involving a fast moving conveyor was the installation of perimeter guarding with access gates protected by a captive key system interlocked with the electrical supply. The system is worthy of wider adoption and is illustrated in Fig 5.

Excavators, draglines and cranes

17   Two persons were killed and 20 sustained major injuries in accidents in this category. A driver was killed when he tried, single-handed, to free a badly

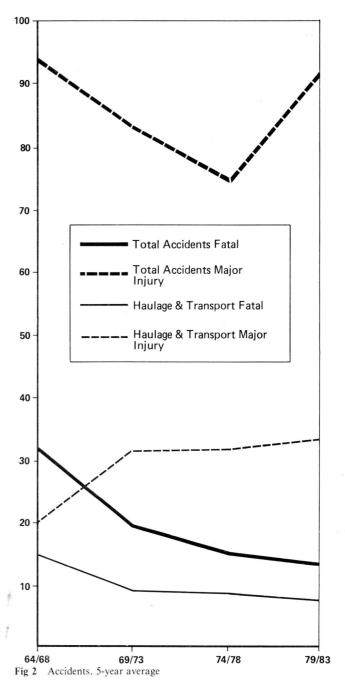

Fig 2   Accidents, 5-year average

frayed drag rope which was trapped in the fair-lead sheave on his dragline excavator. The throttle cable was broken and, with the engine running at maximum operating revs, it would appear that he was drawn round the drag rope drum when the rope was suddenly freed. Apart from emphasising the need for an effective and well documented scheme of maintenance the accident illustrates the dangers involved in attempting to carry out certain types of work unaided. In the past there have been a number of accidents involving excavator drivers who have met with serious injuries when attempting to carry out repairs or adjustments on their own. It is perhaps understandable that they should attempt to do so as they work alone for long periods, but managers should take into account their real capabilities and ensure that firm instructions, preferably in writing, set down work which must not be attempted.

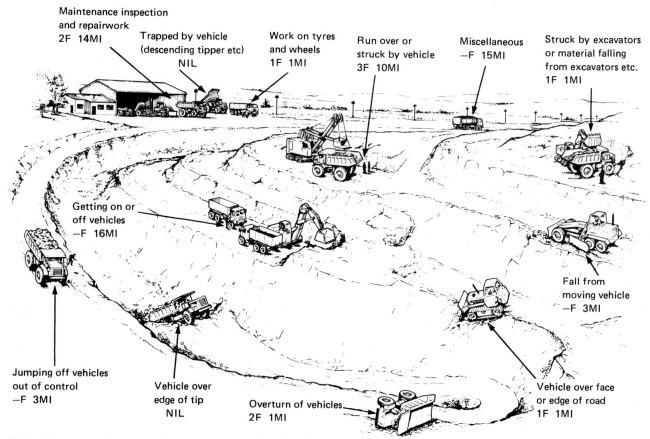

Fig 3 Transport accidents, classified by type and location, 1982–83

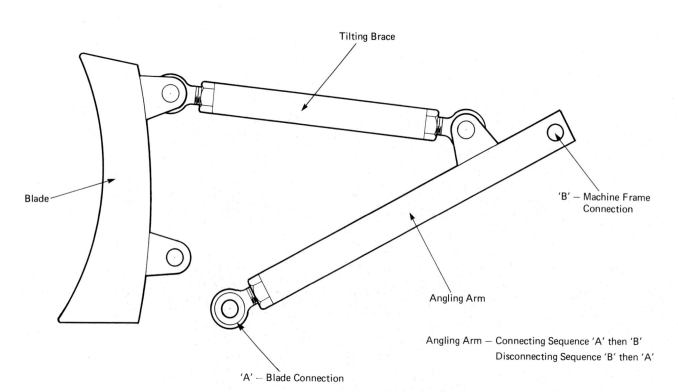

Fig 4 Connection/disconnection of bulldozer angling arm

Fig 5(a) Captive key system
showing control panel

Fig 5(b) Access gate

Other machinery

18 Work on quarry plant and other machinery
resulted in nine accidents being reported. Six of these
accidents occurred when persons were working on
unguarded machinery and on travelling hoppers at
coating plants. Most could probably have been
avoided by improved standards of guarding or the use
of electrical interlocking where appropriate but a need
for more disciplined procedures was also apparent.
One fatal accident involved a contractor's employee
and managers are reminded that they have
responsibility for all persons working at quarries
including contractor's men who may be employed
there. Although contractors may be specialists in their
own work, many have little experience of working in
quarries and should be made fully aware of all aspects
which have a bearing on their safety.

Stumbling, falling or slipping

19 Sixty-three accidents, two of them fatal, were due
to this cause and of these, 24 were caused by falling
from structures, platforms and ladders and 24 from
stationary vehicles and mobile equipment.

20 Most of the accidents relating to structures etc
occurred during maintenance, erection and demolition
where the work often involved removal of sections of
flooring or fencing or necessitated men working in
positions removed from normal walkways and
platforms. Careful supervision can help to reduce the
number of these accidents but proper planning of the
work is most important so that the work is carried out
in a sequence to minimise the exposure to hazard.
Seven of the accidents involved falls from ladders
which is a common cause of accidents in all industries
and attention is drawn to HSE Guidance Note GS 31:

Safe use of ladders, step-ladders and trestles, HMSO, ISBN 0 11 883594 7 which gives much useful information. One improvement over the portable ladder is a fixed steel ladder, but some of these, particularly when vertical, can be potentially hazardous especially to maintenance personnel carrying tools. As an alternative a spiral stairway can often be fitted and when equipped with proper handrails it provides safe access.

21 The majority of stumbling, falling, slipping accidents from stationary vehicles occurred to persons climbing on or off or carrying out maintenance. Of necessity, windscreens and cab windows must be cleaned and secure hand and foot holds are essential for some of these tasks to be carried out safely. Vehicle manufacturers have a part to play in their provision. Two accidents involved drivers who fell from narrow cat walks on the top of dust tankers and much useful advice is provided in HSE Guidance Note GS 26 *Access to road tankers*, ISBN 0 11 883566 1, published by HMSO.

Fires and explosions

22 Four persons were injured in fires and explosions. In two separate incidents fuel oil was used to re-kindle solid fuel stoves and five men were burnt, two seriously, when the vapour exploded. The dangers associated with this type of action should be well known. In another accident a man, using oxy-acetylene equipment to dismantle a raft made up of empty steel drums, was burnt when one of the drums exploded; it was found that it had formerly contained tolulene. HSW Booklet No 32, *Repairs of drums, small tanks etc*, provides much valuable advice on the steps to be taken in similar situations.

Electricity

23 There were seven major injury accidents involving the use of electricity of which six were due to electricians deliberately working on live apparatus. In one accident an electrician used an oscilloscope to check the output wave from an electronic speed controller and initiated a short circuit flashover with the test probes. He had followed procedures in the manufacturer's handbook, which has since been amended. With complex power control systems such as thyristor drives, where oscilloscopes may be essential for fault finding, provision should be made for their safe use. Suitable equipment is available, for permanent installation in power apparatus, to convert the live circuits to be tested into low level voltage signals. Access to these low voltage test points can be arranged without need to open the power system enclosure. Internal points can be monitored as necessary and, with the aid of a suitable interface, the signals can be viewed on an oscilloscope without need to disconnect the oscilloscope earth.

24 In the other accident a plant attendant sustained a fractured skull when he attempted to start a crusher and the oil-filled starter exploded. Severe arcing at a rotor circuit connection within the starter had caused 'cracking' of the oil giving rise to an accumulation of flammable gases in the free volume which was ignited by the arcing. Several accidents and fires in the past have resulted from failures of oil-filled apparatus and oil free types are preferable. Where oil-filled apparatus is used it should be provided with effective electrical protection and safeguarded against overheating. It is vital that the apparatus be properly maintained and the level and quality of the oil regularly checked.

Dangerous occurrences

25 There were 124 dangerous occurrences reported during the two-year period; 33 of these arose from overturning of cranes etc, and 44 from the projection of material outside quarry boundaries from shot firing operations. Details of dangerous occurrences since the introduction of the Notification of Accidents and Dangerous Occurrences Regulations 1980 are shown in Table 2.

26 In incidents connected with cranes and excavators etc, six involved excavators which fell due to collapse of the face edge under the weight of the machine and it is likely that all could have been avoided had they been positioned with tracks at right angles to the working face. The majority of the other incidents were due to failure of ropes and other components and it is apparent that, in addition to the statutory test requirements, managers should institute systematic inspection and maintenance procedures for all excavators, cranes and other lifting machines taking into account the amount of work which is done by the machines.

27 Of the 44 incidents of projected rock from shot firing operations 31 involved distances in excess of 200m and, in one instance, 800m. The number and extent of these incidents, together with the potential dangers both to the general public and to persons employed at the quarry, are a matter of concern. The apparent cause, in most cases, was failure to estimate the true position of the shothole in relation to the face and more accurate alignment of drill rigs together with measurement of face profiles in front of the shot holes is necessary. In a number of instances 'one-off' trimming shots or horizontal shot holes fired in conjunction with a main face blast had been the cause of the projection. It is sometimes claimed, following such incidents, that the projection was due to a hidden fault or discontinuities which could not be foreseen, but investigations have shown that the cause is usually one of faulty operational procedures. In some, the projection can be attributed to variations in the face line which have reduced the intended burden or to deviation of the shot hole which either reduces the burden or results in shot holes being in close proximity at the foot of the face. Managers should devote time to the planning and design of shot firing patterns and to the accurate alignment of shot holes and placement of the explosive. Ideally, benches should not be much higher than 12m to enable adequate inspections to be

Table 2 Dangerous occurrences at quarries		1981	1982	1983
	Collapse or overturning of any hoist, crane, excavator or mobile powered access platform	12	17	16
	Explosion, collapse or bursting of any closed vessel	2	—	1
	Electrical short circuit or overload attended by fire or explosion	1	2	3
	An explosion or fire on any plant or place which resulted in a stoppage of more than 24 hours	6	5	3
	The uncontrolled release of a substance or agent	4	3	2
	The ignition or explosion of explosives where the ignition or explosion was not intentional	2	—	—
	The ignition of anything in a pipe-line, or of anything which immediately before it was ignited was in a pipe-line	1	—	1
	Collapse of any load bearing structure which carries plant, storage hoppers or access way	3	2	1
	The sinking or overturning of any waterborne craft or hovercraft	4	—	1
	An incident in which a person suffers injury resulting from blasting (not being notifiable) and receives treatment at the quarry	1	2	1
	Projection of rock beyond the quarry boundary as a result of blasting operations	18	24	20
	An incident in which a person suffers electric shock or burns requiring treatment at the quarry	4	3	3
	Any movement of material, fire or other event that indicates a tip is, or is likely to become insecure (Part I of the M & Q (Tips) Act 1969 applies)	13	10	4
		71	**68**	**56**

Source: Health and Safety Executive

carried out and to give better control over rock slope stability and drilling and blasting operations. Too much reliance should not be placed on persons who are working to standard patterns which they may change to suit prevailing circumstances without the approval of the manager. When short delay electric detonators are used, particularly in multi-row shots, care should be taken in setting out the delay sequence to ensure that there is not an extended period between adjacent holes. Where because of the proximity and location of property, there is a real risk of projected material, measures such as altering the direction of advance or the use of blast mats may be advisable.

28   Of the 15 dangerous occurrences involving movement of tips and lagoons there were three instances when tipped material slipped onto public highways and, on another occasion, onto a railway line. In the other incidents tipped material moved into working areas. The primary cause in a number of cases appeared to be a failure to obtain competent advice before embarking on tipping operations. Most slope failures occurred on tips of clayey refuse, in some instances where tipping ceased up to 20 years earlier, an indication that degradation can occur with time. Experience has shown that under the best conditions side slopes of this type of refuse should be dressed to a gradient of 1:2½ or less to ensure stability and good practice dictates that frequent and regular inspections should be made and any fissures filled without delay.

29   The potential instability of weak materials is illustrated by the case of a disused lagoon of solidified slurry which, over a period of five years, had been over-tipped with refuse. A final 1 to 1.5m thickness of soil forming material was tipped, during some four weeks, to restore the site. The added load compressed the soft saturated silt creating water pressure leading to bank failure. The loading of wet clayey material, both natural and tipped, will result in water pressure within the wet mass equivalent to nearly the whole of the added load unless the mass can drain. This water pressure causes buoyancy which reduces the resistance to sliding. The concept of creating water pressure through loading is extremely important where bulk tipping is carried out over short, intermittent periods as, during the dormant periods, the exposed surface can weather and absorb water, unless compacted. Any further loading will initiate movement which can only be prevented by buttressing the toe and providing drainage paths for water squeezed out by the new load. Competent technical advice should be sought whenever over-tipping is proposed or where it is intended to change the nature of the tipped material.

30   Two incidents of collapse of load bearing structures involved aggregate storage hoppers. These are particularly vulnerable as they have high centres of gravity, often hold abrasive material and are subject to vehicular damage. Special attention is therefore required to their design, construction and safeguarding particularly as bracing to stiffen the hopper supports is

desirable but cannot always be used in the most efficient way because of the necessity for vehicular access. With the large vehicles used in quarries, heavy impact loads may be experienced and, even if the hopper does not collapse immediately, may cause distortion which could lead to sudden collapse at a later date under minor impact or by increased loading as the hopper is filled. Protection such as plinths, barriers or guide kerbs, should be provided for the supports and any impact damage should be rectified without delay. Once a hopper has been properly erected no bracing or bolts should be removed as the failure of a bolt, especially one in tension, will overload adjacent bolts and could result in accelerating collapse. Regular inspections should be carried out to check for corrosion or damage and remedial measures instituted where necessary.

31 Modern structural design aims to achieve economy by stressing all members fully. This eliminates the traditional reserve of strength in the structures which were designed before computing and drafting facilities became as sophisticated as they are today. The more precise the design, the more important it is for the user of the structure to know the loading limits imposed by the designer and to ensure that loading is kept strictly within those limits. If a structure has been designed by a competent firm, or is of a standard design with clearly laid down loading limits, further enquiry will usually be unnecessary, but if not, the managers should ensure that the structure is adequate for its purposes and has a reasonable factor of safety. No modification, additional loading or variation in loading of a structure from the original design should take place without prior approval, from a person competent to judge the proposal.

32 Although the statutory daily inspection of every working place should reveal any damage to structures, the effects of corrosion, missing bolts or spillage loading may be over-looked. Inspection directed specifically at structures should include checks for any corrosion or other deterioration and the detailing of any damage and necessary remedial action. It should also be directed at confirming that the strength remains adequate for the purpose for which the structure was built, or is being used, whichever is the greater.

33 There were 11 dangerous occurrences in the two categories involving electrical equipment and five were caused by men working on live apparatus. In one of these an experienced electrical surveyor employed by an insurance company sustained superficial electric arc burns to both hands while attempting to carry out statutory electrical tests inside a 440V switch. He forgot to isolate the incoming power supply and initiated a short circuit when he contacted live conductors. This incident highlights the importance of isolation procedures and permit to work schemes.

Health

Noise

34 In October 1983 the Health and Safety Commission launched a campaign with the object of stimulating action in reducing high noise levels at the workplace and protecting employees from their harmful effect. Although prolonged exposure to high levels can result in serious impairment of hearing the effects of noise are still not fully appreciated by many in the industry. Quite apart from irreparable hearing damage, high noise levels can lead to lack of concentration with an adverse effect on safety.

35 A recent survey carried out by HM Inspectors on quarry vehicles and operator's positions on processing plant indicated some typical noise levels.

Machine	Leq
Tertiary crusher	105dB(A)
Primary/secondary crusher	99dB(A)
Coating plant	85dB(A)
Loading shovels	87–90dB(A)
Dump trucks	85–90dB(A)
Medium excavator	87dB(A)
Bulldozers	90–102dB(A)

36 The Department of Employment booklet *Code of Practice for reducing the exposure of employed persons to Noise* SBN 11 360887 X was published by HMSO in 1972. It stipulates a sound level not exceeding 90dB(A) if exposure is to a reasonably steady sound and is continued for 8 hours in any one day. An equivalent value may be calculated if the sound level fluctuates and/or exposure is for a period other than 8 hours. For instance, at a recorded level of 102dB(A), the maximum exposure period, without ear protection, is 30 minutes. However, 90dB(A) ought not to be regarded as a 'safe level' and every effort should be made to reduce the noise level at the operator's ear to as low a level as is reasonably practicable. Reducing the sound level at source is the best and preferred solution but it may not be immediately practicable in some quarry locations. However, there are methods that can be adopted and the HSE book *100 Practical Applications of Noise Reduction Methods,** published as part of the noise campaign, gives much useful information.

37 The provision of hearing protection can help and various forms are available. They are particularly useful when persons have to work in high noise levels for short periods but should not be seen as an alternative to properly engineered sound control measures. To be fully effective it is necessary that ear defenders are properly fitted and, in addition, cleanliness in their use and storage is essential to avoid the risk of ear infection. Sound insulated control cabins provide a solution where operators have to

*HMSO, ISBN 0 11 883691 9

spend the bulk of the shift at one point and tests have indicated that sound levels inside a well constructed cabin can be 20dB(A) less than those immediately outside.

38　In nearly all cases there are some practical steps which can be taken to reduce the health hazard from high noise levels, but these involve an appreciation of the problem and a willingness on the part of all concerned to get to grips with it. Managers and owners of quarries should institute noise reduction programmes, including surveys, to identify the problem areas, and the adoption of remedial measures using expert advice where necessary. High noise zones should be clearly marked and persons not allowed to work in them unless they are wearing ear protection. Contrary to popular belief one does not get used to high noise levels; one becomes deaf.

Airborne dust

39　It is perhaps true to say that whilst dust is recognised as a nuisance which should be controlled the dangerous effects of exposure to concentrations of some respirable dusts over a long period are not always fully appreciated. The increase in production in recent decades may have resulted in men being exposed to increased concentrations of respirable dust and the results of sampling carried out by HM Inspectorate have indicated that more effort needs to be directed toward dust control.

40　The first essential, where a dust hazard may exist, is to carry out a systematic programme of sampling the working environment. Some companies are already carrying out this work and have their own sampling instruments and laboratory facilities for analysis of the samples. Many small quarry companies may not have the staff or facilities available to carry out their own sampling programmes but a number of specialist firms are prepared to provide this service. It may be that arrangements could be explored for companies to group together and share laboratory and sampling facilities and trade associations may have a part to play in making these arrangements.

41　Generally speaking, operatives move about during the course of their work rather than remain in one fixed location, so that personal, rather than fixed point samplers will give a more accurate indication of exposure. Any sample taken, is of course, only an indication of the conditions prevailing at that particular time and may vary widely due to climatic conditions, variations in production throughput and the effectiveness of any dust suppression or collection equipment in use. It is therefore essential in any monitoring programme to ensure that sampling covers as long a period as possible and is carried out under varying conditions in order that an accurate assessment can be made of operator exposure.

42　Respirators are a useful line of defence where men may have to enter a dust laden atmosphere for comparatively short periods of time but should not be seen as an acceptable alternative to effective dust control. Various types of respirator are available but they should be suitable for the prevailing conditions of use and meet an appropriate British Standard.

43　Where necessary, a regular chest X-ray scheme should be instituted and advice on this is available from the HSE Medical Division or the National Coal Board Radiography Units.

Asbestos

44　The dangers associated with the inhalation of asbestos fibres are well known but although the material is not now widely used in the quarrying industry the material may be present at older plants, e.g. in the form of lagging on coating units or binder tanks. The potential danger arises if the fibres are released and then inhaled. If the material can be painted or sealed and is in a position where it cannot be damaged or abraded it may be better to 'leave well alone'. Specialist contractors should be employed where it is necessary to remove or dispose of asbestos.

45　The current control limits for the various types of asbestos together with the new limits effective from 1 August 1984 are shown in Table 3. These control limits are for measurements over a four-hour period and represent the upper limits of permitted exposure, as determined by personal sampling, and are additional to the obligation to reduce exposure to as low a level as is reasonably practicable.

Table 3　Asbestos control limits

Asbestos type	Control limits (fibre/ml)	
	Current	wef 1 Aug 1984
Chrysotile (white asbestos)	1.0	0.5
Amosite (brown asbestos)	0.5	0.2
Crocidolite (blue asbestos)	0.2	0.2

Toxic fumes and gases

46　It has been noted that at some quarries little direct ventilation is provided in welding bays and it may not be generally appreciated that welding processes give rise to the emission of toxic fumes and gases. The flux of some open arc welding rods contain titanium dioxide and fluorides and, in addition, the material being welded may also influence the type and quantity of emission. One or more of the following toxic gases could be given off during arc welding or cutting operations and, in poorly ventilated buildings or confined spaces, could well create a hazard to health:
— Carbon monoxide;
— Carbon dioxide;
— Nitrogen dioxide;
— Ozone;
— Hydrogen fluoride;
— Sulphur dioxide

47 The control and extraction of fumes and gases can be achieved by localised ventilation which should be planned so that the general airflow is away from the operator's face. Periodic checks should be made to test the effectiveness of the system. Where welding operations have to be carried out in very confined spaces with restricted access to outside atmosphere it may be necessary to provide the operator with a special helmet fitted with an independent air supply.

Bitumens, fluxing oils and solvents

48 Hazards can arise in the handling of bitumens, fluxing oils and solvents namely:
(a) Burns due to high storage temperatures of bitumen.
(b) Fires/explosions owing to the flammable nature of the products.
(c) Inhalation of noxious vapours.
(d) Skin diseases.

49 Burns from high temperature material normally involve road tanker drivers and occur during discharge of bitumen into storage tanks and usually follows failure of flexible hoses or connections. The type of pipe connection used on storage tanks consists of an elliptical flange with open slots and accidents have occurred when the connecting bolts have sprung out of the slots when being tightened to rectify a leak. A simple re-design of the flange to incorporate elongated holes for the bolts instead of the open slots would overcome this hazard. Managers should nominate a person to be present, in addition to the driver, when tankers are being discharged, not only to indicate which tanks have to be filled but also to provide assistance should this become necessary.

50 There have been numerous fires and explosions in bitumen storage tanks or associated pipework due to the ignition of flammable vapours at the top of the tanks caused by smoking, welding or the use of naked flames. The tanks, and a specified area around them, should be designated as 'flame-free' and steps taken to control the emission of flammable vapours by keeping tank hatches secured and by fitting blanking plates on the end of delivery pipes when not in use. Blockages may occasionally occur in pipework and valves and where necessary the pipe or components should be dismantled completely and taken away to a safe area to free the blockage. In some instances blockages could be prevented by modification of the layout or by more effective use of line heaters or lagging. Ignition may also occur when tank contents are taken below the level of the heating elements. Usually a limit switch is fitted to prevent contents being drawn from below a safe level and generally the level should be kept about 200mm above the element to avoid localised overheating. However, it is sound practice to regularly check the effectiveness of this safety device and of the temperature gauges and thermostats.

51 Both straight-run (penetration) and cut-back (blended) bitumen, when heated, may give off vapours such as hydrogen sulphide and inhalation should be avoided. Adequate ventilation should be provided on the tops of storage tanks and hatches kept closed to minimise emission. Where it is necessary to work inside a storage tank it should first be allowed to cool to ambient temperature, checked for the presence of harmful gases and well ventilated before any person is allowed to enter. Air fed breathing apparatus should preferably be worn by persons inside the tank with another person stationed on the outside as an added precaution.

52 Fluxes such as creosote are commonly used in their raw state to cut-back the bitumens in coating plant mixers. Prolonged and repeated contact of cut-back bitumens and fluxes with the skin should be avoided and gloves and other suitable protective clothing should be provided, and worn by persons handling bituminous products. Personnel should be made aware of the need for cleanliness and should be provided with adequate washing facilities.

53 Methylene chloride and similar solvents are widely used in some sections of the quarrying industry and are safe when properly used. Inhalation of the vapour can lead to drowsiness or, in heavy concentrations, render a person unconscious. Adequate ventilation is essential and technical advice should be sought from the suppliers regarding the correct procedures and precautions to be taken before any solvents are used. The atmosphere should be checked at regular intervals and all personnel involved in the handling and use of solvents should be adequately trained and be made aware of the potential hazards.

Electrical engineering

Immobilisation of plant

54 Malfunction or failure of electrical control equipment can, in certain circumstances, result in inadvertent starting of plant. It is essential therefore, when servicing or maintaining machines, that they be isolated from the supply or immobilised in some other effective manner. Reliance for immobilisation should not be placed on ancillary stopping devices such as remote control or latching type emergency stop switches. The proper procedure is to disconnect the drive motor from the supply by switching and locking off the main isolator which ought to be provided for every electric motor.

Hazard from polychlorinated biphenyl insulating fluids

55 Polychlorinated biphenyls (PCBs), used under various trade names, were introduced some 40 years ago as insulants and coolants in certain types of electrical equipment such as transformers and capacitors. The potential toxic and carcinogenic effects of PCB liquids was not at first appreciated and they continued to be used by manufacturers into the 1970s when agreement was reached internationally to prohibit further use.

56 Following a fire at a quarry sub-station during the term of this report a firm of contractors was called to dismantle the fire debris, which included damaged capacitors. The contractors immediately recognised the capacitors as being of the PCB filled type needing special handling precautions and disposal facilities. The incident serves as a reminder that PCB liquid filled equipment may remain in use at sites for many years to come and it is essential to identify and label such equipment to warn persons and draw attention to the following:

(a) That special protective clothing and equipment is needed when handling the liquids.

(b) That toxic fumes are evolved if the liquids are involved in a fire.

(c) That the liquids may only be disposed of by incineration at nominated special disposal sites. The Department of the Environment have published guidance on disposal in Waste Management Paper No 6, *Polychlorinated Biphenyl Waste*.

Lighting

57 It is accepted that a high standard of efficient lighting can create a safer environment. In quarries, static installations are normally used in plant areas, while on haul roads and other vehicle operating areas reliance is placed on vehicle lights augmented by mobile lighting towers. It is important that towers are fitted with a safe means of access for maintenance and repair. While a number of very efficient discharge lamps are now available, the effect of glare should be considered and lighting should be graded so that vehicles do not pass abruptly from intense light to darkness. The IES Lighting Guide for Building and Civil Engineering Sites provides useful guidance.

Mechanical engineering

Skid steer loaders

58 These small, wheeled, loading shovels are designed for work in confined spaces by virtue of their manoeuvrability. The bucket is hinged behind the driver with its movements controlled by foot pedals and the drive wheels move in response to two levers, similar to those of a tracked vehicle, hence the machine can turn very quickly. As the driver must climb over the lowered bucket to and from his seat, vehicles should be stopped with the bucket grounded and engine shutdown before the driver enters or leaves so that he will not accidentally set anything in motion. The driving cab should be guarded to prevent contact with the bucket arms but guarding should not prevent emergency egress from the back or roof of the cab whichever is applicable. As the vehicles can spin-turn, pedestrians should not be in the immediate vicinity of working machines and the Manager's Vehicle Rules should cover the use of these machines. Also drivers should be specially trained in their use.

Derrick cranes

59 Many derrick cranes in use at quarries are now old and have cast iron components vital to safe operation. Breakage of these components has caused sudden failure, the consequences of which can be serious as was highlighted by a fatal accident during 1982/83.

60 The derrick cranes which are of most concern usually employ a single motor to power the hoist and jib ropes through a system of gears. These gears, together with interconnecting clutches and supporting bearing pedestals, may be constructed of cast iron. It is also quite common to have one brake for both drums acting through the gears and not at the drums. Failure of a gear, clutch or pedestal can result in loss of control of either the hoist or luffing motions which can neither be prevented nor partially limited by the driver. Cranes of this type should be thoroughly examined by a suitably skilled person to locate the cast iron components and, if the failure of any components such as dog clutches, gears, bearing pedestals or main supporting frames would cause loss of control, then they should be replaced with others made of material not prone to sudden failure.

Failures of welded structures in mobile plant

61 Reference was made in a previous report to the need for care in the repair of welded structures in vehicles. Failures still continue to occur in the main chassis members of trucks and the booms of loading equipment and are usually associated with poor maintenance or construction. In particular there is often insufficient attention during welding to ensure freedom from deposition faults, proper fusion with the parent metal and prevention of undercutting or overlapping at the edges of any weld. When these requirements are not observed, and other procedural defects occur, fatigue cracking is quite likely to result.

62 When cracks of this nature do occur and repair work is necessary, not only should there be a definition of the nature of the parent metal, welding equipment and control of the work, but welders who have the necessary expertise should be employed. This is particularly relevant when machines have to be assembled on site with major components welded locally. Any such welds in components vital to safety should be non-destructively tested immediately before the machine is first put to work and then at regular intervals thereafter consistent with the amount of use.

Vehicle wheels and tyres

63 Accidents and serious incidents indicate the potential danger during the repair and maintenance of vehicle wheels and tyres. When twin rear wheels of trucks have to be removed the tyres should be deflated before the securing bolts are removed.

64 Before inflation and fitting a tyre to the rim, the wheel should be contained within a secure safety cage.

New developments

Haulage and transport

65 Work has continued in the evaluation of various devices designed as aids to combat the restricted visibility from the driving cabs of some quarry vehicles. Although a number have promising possibilities, experience has indicated that some were not robust enough to withstand the quarrying environment. However, evaluation work on an electronic device fitted to a dump truck had an interesting spin-off when, as part of the trials, accelerometers were attached to a truck chassis. These indicated that vibrations increased rapidly at speeds in excess of 32km/h on unsurfaced roads with possible increased maintenance costs and risk of chassis cracking. The tests resulted in the existing speed limit of 40km/h at the quarry being reduced until improvements were effected in the road surface.

66 At several coal quarries clinometers, to indicate both longitudinal and lateral gradients, have been fitted in vehicles used by supervisory staff to assist in checking haul roads and at one quarry a similar instrument is fitted to a bulldozer. The use of such devices during the construction of quarry haul roads will effect improvements in design and quality of the roads and is to be commended.

Drilling and blasting

67 The danger associated with projected material from shot firing operations has focused attention on means of achieving greater accuracy of drilling and the measurement of quarry faces together with alternative methods to the use of explosives for face trimming and secondary breakage.

68 Trials have been carried out with an instrument to detect the position of a shot hole in relation to the toe of a face. It consists of a transmitting probe which is lowered down the shot hole to about quarry floor level. The signal emitted by the probe is registered on a receiver/measuring instrument positioned near the bottom of the face. In its present form, it entails a man standing near the foot of the face but further developments may improve this aspect of design.

69 A project, funded by the Health and Safety Executive, is being carried out at Doncaster Metropolitan Institute of Higher Education into the orientation and positioning of primary shot holes at quarries and two prototype devices have been developed. The first is a sighting device, fitted to the drill rig, to ensure accurate drilling and the second is a probe which is lowered down the shot hole and used in conjunction with an instrument to show deviation. Results of trials using the instrumentation have been analysed and indicate significant improvements in accuracy of alignment of shot holes. The instruments are shown in Fig 6(a), (b), and (c).

70 It is the practice, at some quarries, to use plastic liners in shot holes so that an/fo explosives can be utilised under wet conditions. Where electric detonators are used there is a risk of premature initiation by an electrostatic charge which may be generated in the prilled an/fo when this is pneumatically loaded into the shot hole. Tests have been carried out by the Research and Laboratory Services Division of HSE into the use of anti-static (conductive) plastic liners which may reduce the hazard. Where it is proposed to pneumatically load an/fo into shot holes fitted with plastic liners and also to use electric detonators for initiation it is recommended that:

(a) only anti-static (conductive) liners are used;

(b) loading equipment is earthed;

(c) the loading hose is completely conductive and electrically connected to the loading equipment, and loading hose with metal spirals must not be used.

71 Although the possibility of an electrostatic charge being created by gravity fed an/fo was not specifically investigated, it is advisable that anti-static (conductive) liners should also be used under these circumstances.

72 While compressed air bags are now widely used for lifting purposes one quarry company is successfully using the bags to bring down sections of rock or overhangs at the top of the quarry face following shot firing. The practice has much to commend it as it reduces the use of explosives. Similarly drop ball machines and impact breakers have largely replaced the use of explosives for secondary breakage of oversize material.

73 A rail loading system which utilises rope haulage to pull wagons under a loading point was found to be subject to variations in speed due to rope stretch and bounce leading to inaccurate loading. The rope haulage has now been replaced by a diesel hydraulic loco which is under remote control from the loading point. The radio control gives a choice of four speeds from less than one, to four miles per hour and the loco is fitted with external emergency stop buttons and an audible warning which is actuated automatically prior to movement.

Prosecutions, prohibition and improvement notices

74 There was one prosecution during the two-year period. It related to a fatal accident where a loading shovel ran over the edge of an inclined haul road killing the driver. Two charges were brought against the quarry company which pleaded guilty to both. The first charge alleged inadequate maintenance relating to the vehicle brakes and the second related to the failure to provide a safety barrier at the open side of the haul road. In presenting his case prosecution counsel said: "that if the brakes of the vehicle were the belt then the

Fig 6(a) Inclination device

Fig 6(b) Inclination device fitted to drill rig

Fig 6(c) Angle logging instrument

provision of safety barriers was the braces". This was reflected in the fines imposed by the magistrates of £500 in respect of the first charge and £750 in respect of the second. Costs of £4000 were awarded.

75 Six immediate prohibition notices were served and all these related to incidents of projected material from shot firing operations. There was one deferred prohibition notice which stipulated a reduction in gradient and other improvements on a haul road at a quarry. No improvement notices were served.

Activities not covered by the Mines and Quarries Act 1954

76 These activities, to which the requirements of the Health and Safety at Work etc Act 1974 apply, comprise landfill sites in working or abandoned quarries, peat workings, on-shore exploratory drilling and dry-batch ready mix concrete plants on quarry premises.

Landfill sites

77 Landfill sites are by far the largest sector of these activities and there were about 1500 sites operating at the end of 1983. Stability of tipped slopes and abandoned rock faces, noxious wastes and landfill gas are some of the problems which arise. The existence of gas at a landfill site is undesirable both from an environmental and safety point of view. It is composed principally of methane (up to 65%) and carbon dioxide but is also contaminated with other gases which are corrosive or give off unpleasant odours. Methane can be explosive at concentrations of between 5 and 15% in air and can also migrate to accumulate in such places as culverts or the basements of properties adjacent to landfill sites. The gas can also present problems in the restoration of a site as it may inhibit plant growth. The introduction of methane drainage conducts the gas to a collection point and prevents unwanted migration. It can be burned there under controlled condiltions but gas from large landfill sites is utilised to provide fuel and during the past two years a number of schemes have been put into practice for firing brick kilns and boilers.

78 One fatal and three major injury accidents occurred at landfill sites. There were no witnesses to the fatal accident but it appears that a bulldozer driver was operating his machine parallel to the top edge of a 2m high tip when he misjudged the distance due to smoke and haze and over-ran the edge. It is good practice for vehicles to be kept well clear of the edge when travelling, particularly in conditions of poor visibility.

79 Three dangerous occurrences were reported. One related to a considerable explosion which occurred on a landfill site for domestic refuse in an old quarry which had previously been the site of a fireworks factory. The incident occurred in the early hours of a Sunday morning and no person was injured but debris from the explosion was deposited far and wide. Investigations showed that chemicals had been deposited in a chamber in the floor of the quarry when the factory was demolished and they provided the source of the explosion. Subsequently the site was excavated and the remaining chemicals removed.

80 It is the practice at some landfill sites to enclose hazardous waste in 'cells' constructed of inert material to limit the quantity of contaminated effluent draining from the site. The cell walls inevitably become retaining banks and must be designed to resist the forces imposed upon them. In a dangerous occurrence at an abandoned clay quarry toxic waste, treated by a proprietory process, was put into cells to solidify. The rate at which the waste gained shear strength varied considerably and one of the cell walls was evidently under excessive hydrostatic loading when it burst, releasing a large quantity of waste into another part of the quarry. Cracks in the wall gave sufficient warning of the impending failure to allow men to be withdrawn. It is advisable when using earth retaining walls that specialist advice is taken on their design and construction.

Exploratory drilling

81 Exploratory drilling for oil, gas and coal continues in various parts of the country and while some of the sites are long term many are of a transitory nature.

82 Before drilling operations are started, zoning limits should be established following an area classification study as laid down in BS5345*. This standard also details the selection, installation and maintenance of electrical apparatus for use in potentially explosive atmospheres. Diesel electric rigs have the advantage that the diesel engines can be sited at some distance from the drill site but many diesel mechanical rigs are still in use. Where diesel engines are to be used in Zone 2 areas, and are not sited in pressurised houses, both the exhaust discharge and air inlet systems must be protected by flame traps located, in the latter case, between the air cleaner and the inlet manifold. Although dry type air filters are preferable, wet filters are acceptable provided that they are designed to use a fire resistant fluid. Any flame trap used must:

* Selection, installation and maintenance of electrical apparatus in potentially explosive atmospheres.

(a) be so mounted that it is protected from accidental damage so far as is practicable;

(b) be so designed and constructed that it may be readily removed as a complete unit for inspection, cleaning and overhaul and that incorrect assembly of the components is not possible;

(c) be constructed of materials resistant to corrosion and abrasion and of adequate strength to minimise the possibility of distortion of component parts.

83 There were 11 major injury accidents during the two-year period, the majority of which were due to slipping or being struck by items of equipment. Lengths of proprietory non-slip matting, which can be hosed down with water, have been used successfully at several drillling sites to reduce the risk of slipping on mud-covered surfaces.

84 In the one dangerous occurrence the operator of a mobile drill rig drove the vehicle with the drill mast in the raised position under an 11 000V overhead cable and fouled the line conductors. He jumped out of the cab to assess the problem and then sustained electric shock, minor burns to his hands and feet and a dislocated shoulder when he attempted to climb back onto the vehicle which was subsequently extensively damaged by fire. The dangers posed by overhead electric lines should be well known and the recommendations made in HSE Guidance Note GS6 *Avoidance of danger from overhead electric lines* should be followed.

Peat workings

85 The excavation of peat continues at a similar level to previous years. An interesting development in the guarding of the specialised machinery used in the peat fields is the installation at two major sites of an interlock system which stops the diesel engine prime mover when the driver leaves his control cab.

86 Trials have been carried out to maintain communication with operatives working on their own in the very extensive workings. Initially CB type radio transceivers were tried but more powerful transceivers, using a discrete frequency and capable of operating over a considerable range, have been found to be more satisfactory.

Dry batch ready mix concrete plants

87 These units are usually extensions of existing quarry plant and no accidents were reported.

Table 4 Quarries: fatal and major injury accidents by type 1979–83

Accident classification	Fatal accidents					Major injury accidents					Fatal and major injury accidents				
	1979	1980	1981	1982	1983	1979	1980	1981	1982	1983	1979	1980	1981	1982	1983
Falls of ground	—	—	1	2	—	3	6	10	3	2	3	6	11	5	2
Explosives	—	1	—	1	—	2	—	1	—	2	2	1	1	1	2
Rail track vehicles	—	—	—	—	—	2	—	—	—	1	2	—	—	—	1
Trackless vehicles	7	10	8	8	1	17	16	25	15	12	24	26	33	23	13
Conveyors	1	—	1	1	3	10	6	10	9	9	11	6	11	10	12
Forward acting and dragline excavators and bucket wheel excavators	—	—	—	1	—	—	1	1	5	7	—	1	1	6	7
Cranes and other lifting equipment	—	—	1	1	—	4	1	3	3	5	4	1	4	4	5
Other machines	—	—	—	2	—	1	3	6	3	4	1	3	6	5	4
Waterborne craft	—	1	1	—	—	—	—	1	—	—	—	1	2	—	—
Stumbling, falling or slipping	3	2	1	1	1	34	20	29	34	27	37	22	30	35	28
Fires and explosions	—	—	—	—	—	3	4	5	3	1	3	4	5	3	1
Electricity	1	—	—	—	—	—	—	—	5	2	1	—	—	5	2
Use of tools and appliances (including flying splinters)	—	1	—	—	—	7	2	8	12	6	7	3	8	12	6
Falling objects	—	—	—	1	—	3	1	4	6	5	3	1	4	7	5
Other accidents	—	2	1	—	—	4	4	2	8	5	4	6	3	8	5
Total reportable accidents	12	17	14	18	5	90	64	105	106	88	102	81	119	124	93

Source: Health and Safety Executive

Table 5 Quarries: fatal and major injury accidents by mineral worked 1979–83

Mineral	Fatal accidents					Major injury accidents				
	1979	1980	1981	1982	1983	1979	1980	1981	1982	1983
Gravel and sand (including silica sand and pig bed sand)	2	3	3	3	—	15	8	18	19	18
Limestone	1	5	4	2	2	18	20	31	25	29
Clay, shale	—	—	—	—	—	—	—	1	1	1
Chalk, chert and flint	—	1	—	1	—	1	1	3	1	—
Ironstone	—	—	—	—	—	1	1	—	—	—
Igneous rock (including felspar)	3	2	2	1	—	15	6	11	20	12
Sandstone (including silica stone and ganister)	1	1	—	1	—	3	1	4	3	1
China clay, china stone, potters' clay, ball clay, mica clay and fireclay	3	—	—	1	1	10	5	2	7	6
Slate	—	—	1	—	—	2	—	2	—	—
Other minerals	—	1	1	2	1	—	3	4	5	6
Opencast coal	2	4	3	7	1	25	19	29	25	15
All minerals	12	17	14	18	5	90	64	105	106	88

Source: Health and Safety Executive

Table 6 Quarries: fatal (F) and major injury (MI) accidents by type and mineral worked

	Limestone		Sand & Gravel		Ig rock		Clay		Coal		Others		Total	
	F	MI	F	MI	F	MI	F	MI	F	MI	F	MI	F	MI
Falls of ground from face	—	—	—	1	—	1	—	—	2	1	—	—	2	3
Falls of ground elsewhere	—	2	—	—	—	—	—	—	—	—	—	—	—	2
Explosives	—	—	—	—	—	—	—	—	—	2	1	—	1	2
Tracked vehicles (rail)	—	1	—	—	—	—	—	—	—	—	—	—	—	1
Rubber tyred load carrying vehicles	—	6	—	3	—	1	—	—	4	5	—	—	4	15
Rubber tyred loaders	1	—	1	1	—	—	—	—	—	—	1	1	3	2
Track mounted loaders and bulldozers	—	—	—	—	—	1	—	—	—	2	1	—	1	3
Scrapers and graders	—	—	—	—	—	—	—	—	—	—	—	3	—	3
Other self propelled vehicles	—	—	—	—	—	1	—	—	1	3	—	—	1	4
Conveyors	2	8	—	6	1	1	—	2	1	—	—	1	4	18
Forward acting and dragline excavators and bucket wheel excavators	—	2	1	1	—	1	—	—	—	8	—	—	1	12
Cranes and other lifting equipment	1	3	—	—	—	2	—	2	—	1	—	—	1	8
Other machines	—	3	1	—	—	3	—	—	1	1	—	—	2	7
Waterborne craft	—	—	—	—	—	—	—	—	—	—	—	—	—	—
SFS* from structures, platforms, ladders	—	7	—	7	—	2	2	1	—	3	—	2	2	22
SFS from stationary vehicles and mobile equipment	—	5	—	6	—	3	—	3	—	5	—	2	—	24
SFS elsewhere	—	3	—	2	—	2	—	6	—	1	—	1	—	15
Fires and explosions	—	1	—	—	—	—	—	—	—	3	—	—	—	4
Use of tools and appliances	—	6	—	2	—	4	—	—	—	5	—	1	—	18
Electricity	—	2	—	2	—	2	—	—	—	1	—	—	—	7
Falling objects	—	1	—	4	—	4	—	—	—	1	1	1	1	11
Other accidents	—	4	—	2	—	4	—	—	—	3	—	—	—	13
Total	4	54	3	37	1	32	2	14	9	45	4	12	23	194

SFS = Stumbling, falling and slipping   *Source: Health and Safety Executive*

Table 7   Quarries: output and employment by mineral worked 1981–82

Mineral	Output (million tonnes)		Employment Direct		Indirect	
	1981	1982	1981	1982	1981	1982
Gravel and sand (including industrial sand)	82.4	83.4	7509	7040	2244	2091
Limestone (including dolomite)	76.8	82.8	7787	6898	2521	2032
Clay, shale	18.8	20.3	886	891	304	343
Chalk, chert and flint	11.8	11.6	893	806	128	107
Ironstone	0.16	0.08	81	24	—	—
Igneous rock	25.3	30.0	3356	3747	993	1230
Sandstone	9.6	10.8	1528	1502	518	412
China clay, ball clay, fire clay, china stone	4.5	4.2	2459	3095	406	512
Slate	0.35	0.8	397	330	89	53
Coal	13.1	14.6	4735	5864	692	788
Gypsum, Fuller's earth, soapstone and talc	3.1	2.9	147	130	26	26
Barytes, fluorspar, metalliferous ores	0.34	0.3	70	110	41	72
Total	246.25	261.78	29848	30437	7962	7666

Source: Business Statistics Office

Printed in the UK for HMSO
Dd 715214 C20 3/85